GW00706040

Baby Names

Baby Names

Over 1,000 inspiring names for your child

Janice Easton-Epner

Photography by Debi Treloar

RYLAND
PETERS
& SMALL
LONDON NEW YORK

Designer *Sarah Walden*
Commissioning Editor *Annabel Morgan*
Picture Researcher *Claire Hector*
Production *Deborah Wehner*
Art Director *Gabriella Le Grazie*
Publishing Director *Alison Starling*

First published in the
United States of America in 2003
by Ryland Peters & Small, Inc
519 Broadway
5th Floor
New York, NY 10012
www.rylandpeters.com

ISBN 1 84172 521 8

Printed and bound in China

Contents

Introduction

Names are so much more than the sum of their letters; they are an expression of our cultural beliefs, personal tastes, and hopes for immortality. Naming a child can be an intense process, meditating on the name and our associations with it, combining that with a glimpse of a hoped-for future. Be playful and optimistic, by all means, but don't forget that whatever name you choose should be able to last a lifetime.

Due to its size, this book cannot claim to be a complete source of names, but it does contain a listing of names popular, traditional, and fanciful that will appeal to the parents of the third millennium. The current trend in names is the creation of original spellings, and this book lists many variants for each name. Also included are nicknames and language variations. If tradition is what you're after, there are biblical names and presidential names. For those interested in something a little more outré, perhaps celebrity names or Shakespearean names will suit your fancy. Further resources for name ideas are suggested as well.

Don't let the name game get you down—make it a pleasant daydream while you await the most exciting moment of your life!

Girl

Aaliyah
Hebrew, Ascender

Adelaide (Addie, Ada)
French, Noble or kind

Adita
African, Basket

Adriana (Adrianna, Adrienne)
Spanish, Dark or rich

Ainsley
Anglo-Saxon, My own meadow

Alana (Alanna, Alaina)
Celtic/Gaelic, Peaceful or serene

Alexandra (Alejandra, Alejandrina, Alexa, Alexia, Alexis)
Greek, Protector of Mankind

Alice (Alicia, Alisha)
Greek, Noble truth

Allison (Alison, Alyson)
German, Noble birth

Amanda (Mandy)
Latin, Worthy of Love

Amy (Aimee)
French, Beloved

Andrea
Latin, Courageous

Angel (Angela, Angelica, Angelina, Angie)
Latin, Angelic

Anita
Latin, Gracious

Ann (Ana, Anna, Annabelle, Anne, Annette, Annie, Antoinette, Antonia)
Hebrew, Blessed with grace

Annika (Annica)
Swedish, Blessed with grace

Anya
Slavic, Variant of Anna

Ariadne (Ariane, Arianna)
Greek, Holy

Ariel
Hebrew, Lion of God

Arlene
Celtic/Gaelic, Pledge

Ashley
Anglo-Saxon, From the ash tree

Audrey
Anglo-Saxon, Noble strength

Ava
Greek, Like a bird

Avery
Anglo-Saxon, Nobility

Bailey (Bailee, Baylee)
Anglo-Saxon, Bailiff or steward

Barbara (Barbie)
Greek, Strange or foreign

Beatrice (Bea)
French, One who brings joy

Bethany
Hebrew, Life, Town near Jerusalem

Beverly
Anglo-Saxon, Near the meadow of the beavers

Blair
Scottish/Gaelic, Field or plain

Blanche (Blanca)
French, White

Bonnie (Bonita)
Latin, Pretty or beautiful

Brandy (Brandi)
American, Warm and comforting

Brenda
German, Sword blade

Brenna
Celtic/Gaelic, Little raven

Bridget
Celtic/Gaelic, Strong

Brianna (Briana, Bryanna)
Celtic/Gaelic, Strong one

Brittany
Anglo-Saxon, From Brittania

Brooke (Brooklyn)
Anglo-Saxon, Brook or stream

Boy

Aaron
Hebrew, Enlightened

Abel
Hebrew, A breath

Abraham
Hebrew, Father of a multitude

Adrian
Latin, Of the Adriatic

Albert (Al, Alberto, Bert)
Teutonic, Noble or bright

Alan (Allan, Allen, Alonzo)
Celtic/Gaelic, Handsome

Alexander (Alejandro, Alex)
Greek, Protector of mankind

Alfonso
Italian, Eager or noble

Alfred (Alfredo)
Anglo-Saxon, Counselor

Alton
Anglo-Saxon, Old town

Alvin
Teutonic, Light-skinned

Amos
Hebrew, Troubled

Andrew (Andre, Andres, Andy)
Greek, Manly or courageous

Angel (Angelo)
Greek, Angelic

Anthony (Tony)
Greek, Praiseworthy

Archie (Archibald)
German, Very bold

Armando
Latin, Of the army

Arnold
German, Strong as an eagle

Arthur (Arturo)
Celtic/Gaelic, A follower of Thor

Aubrey
German, Noble or bright

Austin
German, Revered or exalted

Bailey
Anglo-Saxon, Bailiff or steward

Barry
Celtic/Gaelic, Marksman

Benjamin (Ben, Bennie, Benny)
Hebrew, Son of my right hand

Bernard
French, Bold as a bear

Blake
Anglo-Saxon, Pale

Boyd
Celtic/Gaelic, Blond

Bradford
Anglo-Saxon, A broad Ford

Bradley (Brad)
Anglo-Saxon, A broad meadow

Brandon (Branden, Brendan, Brendon, Brennan)
Celtic/Gaelic, A little raven

Brent
Anglo-Saxon, From high on the hill

Brett (Bret)
Celtic/Gaelic, Briton or British

Brian (Bryan, Bryant)
Celtic/Gaelic, Strong one

Brock
Anglo-Saxon, A badger

Brody
Celtic/Gaelic, Brother

Bruce
French, Woods

Bryson (Bryce)
Anglo-Saxon, Son of a nobleman

Buddy (Bud)
American, Friend

Burt (Burton)
Anglo-Saxon, Town of the Fortress

Byron
Anglo-Saxon, Farm or cottage

Girl

Caitlyn (Caitlin, Kaitlyn, Katelin, Katelyn)
Greek, Pure

Camille
French, Virginal or unblemished character

Camryn (Kamryn)
Celtic/Gaelic, Bent nose

Carol (Carole, Carrie, Kerry)
Latin, Melody or song

Caroline (Carolyn)
Latin, Pretty and joyous song

Casey (Kasey)
Celtic/Gaelic, Brave

Cassandra (Cassie)
Greek, Prophet

Cecilia (Cece, Cecelia, Cecily, Celia)
Latin, Blind

Charlotte (Charlene)
French, Petite and feminine

Chelsea
Anglo-Saxon, Port of ships

Cheryl (Sheryl)
French, Beloved

Cheyenne (Cheyanne)
Native American, People of alien speech

Christina (Christie, Christine, Christy)
Greek, Christ-bearer

Claire (Clara, Clare)
French, Clear or bright

Clarissa
Latin, Brilliant

Claudia
Latin, Female form of Claude, Lame

Colleen
Celtic/Gaelic, Girl

Courtney
Anglo-Saxon, From the court

Cynthia (Cindy)
Greek, The moon personified

Dakota
Native American, Tribal name

Dana
Anglo-Saxon, From Denmark

Danielle (Daniela)
French, God is my judge

Darlene
French, Little darling

Deanna
Latin, Divine valley

Deborah (Debbie, Debra)
Hebrew, The bee

Deja
French, Before

Delaney
Celtic/Gaelic, Descendant of the challenger

Delilah
Hebrew, Hair or poor

Delia
Greek, Girl from the isle of Delos

Denise
Female form of Dennis

Denver
American, Green valley

Desiree
French, Desired

Destiny (Destinee)
American, For which you were meant to do

Diana (Diane, Dianna, Dianne)
Greek, Divine

Dinah (Dina)
Hebrew, God has judged

Donna
Latin, Lady or woman

Doris
Greek, Wealth of the sea

Dorothy (Dotty)
Greek, Gift of God

Boy

Cade
American, Pure

Caden
American, Fighter

Caleb
Hebrew, Faithful or bold

Calvin
Latin, Bald

Cameron
Celtic/Gaelic, Bent nose

Carl (Carlos, Carlton, Karl)
Teutonic, Strong one

Carson (Carsyn)
Anglo-Saxon, Son of Carr

Casey
Celtic/Gaelic, Brave

Cesar
Latin, Long-haired one

Chandler
Anglo-Saxon, Candle-maker

Charles (Charlie)
Teutonic, Manly or farmer

Chase
Anglo-Saxon, Hunter

Christian (Chris, Kristian)
Anglo-Saxon, Of the Christian faith

Christopher (Kristopher)
Greek, Christ-bearer

Clayton (Clay)
Anglo-Saxon, Town on clay land

Cody
Anglo-Saxon, A cushion

Colby
Anglo-Saxon, Dark-haired

Cole
Teutonic, Dark and swarthy

Colin (Collin)
Anglo-Saxon, Child

Colton
Anglo-Saxon, Coal town

Conrad (Connor, Conner)
Teutonic, Bold or wise counselor

Cooper
Anglo-Saxon, Barrel maker

Corey (Cory)
Celtic/Gaelic, The hollow

Dalton
Anglo-Saxon, The town near the valley

Devin (Devan, Deven, Devon)
Anglo-Saxon, Poet

Damian (Damien)
Greek, Sweet and harmless

Diego
Spanish, Saint James

Daniel (Dan, Dana, Dane, Danny)
Hebrew, God is my judge

Dominick (Dominic)
Latin, Belonging to God

Dante
Latin, Lasting

Donald (Don, Donnie)
Celtic/Gaelic, World leader

Darius
Greek, Wealthy

Donovan (Duncan)
Celtic/Gaelic, Dark warrior

Darryl (Darrel, Darrell, Daryl)
French, Dear or beloved

Douglas (Doug)
Celtic/Gaelic, Flowing from the
dark river

David (Dave, Davis)
Hebrew, Beloved

Drake
Anglo-Saxon, Dragon

Dawson
Anglo-Saxon, Son of David

Drew
Greek, Manly and courageous

Dennis
Greek, Wild or frenzied

Dustin (Dusty)
Anglo-Saxon, Warrior

Derrick (Derek)
Anglo-Saxon, Famous ruler

Dylan (Dillon)
Welsh, Born from the ocean

Flower & Tree Names

Celebrate the spirit of life and name your child for nature's beauty. While names like Daisy and Hyacinth are clearly flowers, other names like Chaney, Whitley, or Zuza may appeal to those with less interest in the outdoors. Whichever you choose, they are sure to perennially delight!

Girl

Daisy
American, For the daisy flower

Fern
Anglo-Saxon, Fern-like

Geranium
Greek, Of the geranium flower

Holly
British, Holly grove

Hyacinth (Jacinta, Jacintha)
Greek, Young and beautiful

Myrtle
Greek, The tree or victory

Oleander
Greek, An evergreen tree

Peony
Latin, Healing

Poppy
Old English, Remembrance

Rodanthe
Greek, Rose

Rosemarie (Rosemary)
French, Bitter rose

Verbena
Latin, A sacred bough or plant

Violet
Latin, Violet flower

Whitley
Anglo-Saxon, White meadow

Willow
Anglo-Saxon, Freedom or tree

Zinnia
Latin, From the flower

Zuza
Slavic, Graceful lily

Boy

Ashton
Anglo-Saxon, Ash tree grove

Acton
Anglo-Saxon, From the settlement
with oak trees

Barclay
Anglo-Saxon, From the meadow of
the birch trees

Barlow
Anglo-Saxon, From the barley hill

Chaney (Cheyney)
Old French, From the oak grove

Dagan
Hebrew, Grain

Ewan
Scottish/Gaelic, Born of the
yew tree

**Forrest (Forest,
Forrester, Forster)**
Old French, Out of the woods

Griswold
Teutonic, From the gray forest

Hadden
Anglo-Saxon, Child of the heather-
filled valley

Lindsey (Lindsay)
British, Linden trees near the
water

Myall
Aboriginal, A wild acacia tree

Narcissus
Greek, The flower

Ogden
Anglo-Saxon, From the valley of
oak trees

Sage
British, Prophet

Girl

Ebony
Anglo-Saxon, Dark beauty

Echo
Greek, Sound returned

Eden
Hebrew, Paradise

Edith
Teutonic, Rich gift

Edna
Hebrew, Pleasure or delight

Eileen (Aileen)
Celtic/Gaelic variant of Helen,
Bringer of light

Elaine
French, Light

Eliana (Alaina, Alayna)
French, Fair one

Elisa
Spanish, Dedicated to God

Elissa (Alyssa)
Greek, Queen of Carthage

**Elizabeth (Bessie, Beth, Betsy,
Betty, Eliza, Libby, Lizzie)**
Hebrew, Consecrated to God

Ella
Anglo-Saxon, Beautiful fairy woman

Ellen (Elena)
Greek, Light

Eloise
French, Battle maiden

Elsa (Elsie)
Teutonic, Consecrated to God

Elvira
Latin, Impartial judgment

Emily (Amelia, Emely)
Latin, Industrious

Emma
German, Universal

Erica (Erika)
Latin, Honorable ruler

Erin
Celtic/Gaelic, Peace

Ernestine
Teutonic, Fight to the finish

Esmeralda
Spanish, Emerald

Estelle
Latin, Star

Ethel
Teutonic, Noble

Eudora
Greek, Wonderful gift

Fannie (Fanny)
Anglo-Saxon, French person

Fatima
Arabic, Weaning; daughter of
Muhammad

Fawn (Fawne)
Old French, Young deer

Faye
French, Fairy or elf

Eula
Greek, Fair of speech

Felicia
Latin, Happy

Eunice
Greek, Good or noble victory

Felicity (Felicite)
Latin, Lucky or fortunate

Evelyn
Celtic/Gaelic, Life

Fiona
Celtic/Gaelic, White or fair

Faith
Latin, Trust or faith

Florence (Flora)
Latin, Blooming

Francis (Francine)
Latin, From France

Francesca
Latin, Free

Freda (Frieda)
German, Peaceful

Boy

Eamon
Celtic/Gaelic, Protector

Emmanuel (Emanuel)
Hebrew, God is with us

Earl
Anglo-Saxon, A nobleman

Enrique
Portuguese/Spanish, The rule of the home

Earnest (Ernest, Ernesto)
Teutonic, The serious, earnest one

Eric (Erick, Erik)
Old Norse, Honorable ruler

Edgar
Anglo-Saxon, Great spearman

Ervin
Scottish, From Irvington

Edmund (Edmond, Eduardo)
Anglo-Saxon, Prosperous protector

Ethan
Hebrew, Firm or strong

Edward (Ed, Eddie)
Anglo-Saxon, Happy guardian

Eugene
Greek, Born lucky

Edwin
Anglo-Saxon, Prosperous friend

Evan
Welsh, Young warrior

Efrain
Spanish, Fruitful

Everett (Everet)
Anglo-Saxon, As strong as a boar

Elbert
Teutonic, Noble and illustrious

Fagan
Celtic/Gaelic, The little fiery one

Eldon
Anglo-Saxon, From the hill

Fairley (Farley)
Anglo-Saxon, A clearing in the woods

Elijah (Eli, Elias, Elliot, Elliott, Ellis)
Hebrew, The Lord is God

Faisal (Faysal)
Arabic, A wise judge

Elmer
Anglo-Saxon, Famous

Fallon
Celtic/Gaelic, A leader

Emil (Emilio, Emmett)
Teutonic, Industrious

Felix
Latin, Happy and prosperous

Fenwick
Anglo-Saxon, From the farm in the marshland

Fernando
Spanish, Daring and adventurous

Ferris
Celtic/Gaelic, A rock

Finian
Celtic/Gaelic, Fair or white

Fletcher
Old French, Arrow maker

Flint
Anglo-Saxon, Hard stone

Florian
Latin, A flower blooming

Floyd
Welsh, The hollow

Flynn
Celtic/Gaelic, The red-haired one

Ford
Anglo-Saxon, River crossing

Francis (Francisco)
Latin, From France

Frank (Frankie)
Teutonic, A member of the tribe of Franks

Franklin
Old French, Free man

Frederick (Fred, Freddie, Freddy, Fredrick)
Teutonic, A peaceful ruler

Girl

Gabrielle (Gabriela, Gabriella)
Hebrew, God is my strength

Gail (Gayle)
Anglo-Saxon, Gay or lively

Geneva
French, Juniper berry

Genevieve
French, White wave

Georgia (Georgina)
Greek, Female form of George or farmer

Gigi
French, A girl from the farm

Gilda
Teutonic, A sacrifice

Gillian (Jillian)
Latin, Youthful

Gina
Italian, Garden

Ginger
Latin, Ginger plant

Giovana
Italian, God is gracious

Giselle
French, A promise

Gladys
Welsh, Lame

Glenda
Celtic/Gaelic, Divine goddess

Gloria
Latin, Glory

Grace
Latin, Grace

Guadalupe
Spanish, Mother of God

Gwendolyn (Gwen)
Celtic/Gaelic, White brow

Hailey (Hailee, Haleigh, Haley, Halle, Haylee, Hayley)
Anglo-Saxon, Hero

Hannah (Hanna)
Hebrew, Grace of God

Harley
Anglo-Saxon, Spacious meadow

Harriet (Hattie)
Teutonic, Home ruler

Hazel
Anglo-Saxon, Commander

Heather
Anglo-Saxon, Heather

Heaven
American, From the heavens

Heidi
German, Noble or kind

Helen (Helena)
Greek, Bright one

Henrietta
German, Female form of Henry

Hermione
Greek, Handsome one

Hope
Anglo-Saxon, Hopeful or optimistic

Hunter
Anglo-Saxon, One who hunts

Imelda
Spanish, A floret

Imogene (Imogen)
Latin, Image

Ines (Inez)
Spanish, Gentle

Irene
Greek, Peace

Iris
Greek, The rainbow

Irma (Erma)
Latin, God of war

Isabel (Isabella)
Spanish, Consecrated to God

Ivana
Hebrew, God is gracious

Ivy
Greek, Ivy plant

Boy

Gabriel (Gabe)
Hebrew, Hero of God

Gareth
Welsh, Gentle

Gary (Garret, Garrett, Garry)
Anglo-Saxon, To watch

Gavin
Welsh, Little hawk

Gene
Anglo-Saxon, Born to nobility

George
Greek, Farmer

Gerard (Gerald, Gerardo, Jerald)
French, Brave

Gilbert (Gilberto)
Anglo-Saxon, Trusted

Giovanni
Italian, God is gracious

Glen (Glenn)
Celtic/Gaelic, Secluded woody valley

Gordon
Anglo-Saxon, Round hill

Grady
Celtic/Gaelic, Of high rank

Graham
Anglo-Saxon, Home in a graveled valley

Gregory (Greg, Gregg)
Greek, Vigilant watchman

Griffin
Greek, Mythological beast

Guillermo
Spanish, Form of William

Guy
Latin, Living spirit

Harley
Anglo-Saxon, Spacious meadow

Harold (Harry)
Nordic, Army ruler

Ian
Celtic/Gaelic, God is gracious

Harvey
French, Army warrior

Ignatius (Ignacio)
Anglo-Saxon, Fiery one

Hayden
Anglo-Saxon, The rosy meadow

Ira
Hebrew, Watchful descendant

Hector
Greek, Anchor or steadfast

Irving
Anglo-Saxon, Handsome and fair

Hedley
Anglo-Saxon, Clearing in heather

Isaac
Hebrew, He will laugh

Henry (Henri)
Teutonic, Ruler of the home

Isaiah
Hebrew, Salvation by God

Herbert (Herb)
Teutonic, Excellent army ruler

Ismael (Ismail)
Hebrew, God will hear

Herman
Teutonic, Person of high rank

Ivan
Slavic, God is good

Holden
Anglo-Saxon, Hollow in the valley

Homer
Greek, Promise

Houston
Celtic/Gaelic, Town of houses

Hugh (Hugo)
German, Bright in mind and spirit

Shakespearean Names

Is there any poet, playwright, or author more revered than the Bard of Avon? Here is a brief selection of the unusual names found within his many plays.

Girl

Bianca
(*Othello, The Taming of the Shrew*)
Latin, White or fair-skinned

Cordelia
(*King Lear*) Anglo-Saxon, Daughter
of the sea

Hero
(*Much Ado About Nothing*) Greek,
Brave Defender

Juliet
(*Romeo & Juliet*) French, Soft-haired

Luciana
(*The Comedy of Errors*) Italian, Light

Mariana
(*Measure for Measure*) French,
Bitterly wanted child

Miranda
(*The Tempest*) Latin, Miraculous

Nell
(*The Comedy of Errors*)
Greek, Stone

Ophelia
(*Hamlet*) Greek, A helper

Paulina
(*A Winter's Tale*) Latin, Little one

Portia
(*The Merchant of Venice*)
Latin, Name of a Roman clan

Rosalind
(*As You Like It*) Spanish, Fair rose

Timandra
(*Timon of Athens*)
Greek, Maiden of honor

Titania
(*A Midsummer Night's Dream*)
Greek, The great one

Viola
(*Twelfth Night*)
Italian, Fragrant of violets

Boy

Adrian
(*The Tempest*)
Latin, Of the Adriatic

Angus
(*Macbeth*) Celtic/Gaelic, Unique

Barnardo
(*Hamlet*) Teutonic, Bold as a bear

Benvolio
(*Romeo & Juliet*) Italian, Well-wished

Caliban
(*The Tempest*) Greek, Devoted man

Cornelius
(*Cymbeline*) Latin, Horn-colored

Duncan
(*Macbeth*) Celtic/Gaelic, Dark-skinned warrior

Horatio
(*Hamlet*) Latin, Hour in time

Lennox
(*Macbeth*) Scottish/Gaelic, From a Scottish district and surname

Lysander
(*A Midsummer Night's Dream*) Greek, One who is freed

Montano
(*Othello*) Italian, Large hill

Oberon
(*A Midsummer Night's Dream*)
Teutonic, Bear heart

Paris
(*Romeo & Juliet*)
Greek, Protector of men

Petruchio
(*The Taming of the Shrew*)
Italian, Great stone

Prospero
(*The Tempest*)
Italian, Lucky or fortunate

Seton
(*Macbeth*)
Anglo-Saxon, A place by the sea

Yorick
(*Hamlet*) Greek, A tiller of the soil

Girl

Jasmine (Jasmin, Jazmin, Jazmine)
Persian, Jasmine flower

Jayden
American, God has heard

Jayla
American, Happy

Jean (Jeanne, Jeannie)
Hebrew, Female form of Jebediah

Jeannette (Jeanette)
French, God's grace

Jacquelyn (Jackie)
French, One who supplants

Jada (Jayda)
American, Wise

Jaden (Jadyn)
Hebrew, God has heard

Jane (Jana, Janelle, Janet, Janie, Janine)
Hebrew, God is gracious

Janice (Jan, Janis)
Hebrew, God's gracious gift

Jennifer (Jenna, Jennie, Jenny)
Anglo-Saxon, Fair spirit

Jessica (Jessie)
Hebrew, God sees

Jill
Latin, Girl

Jocelyn
Latin, Light heard

Jody (Jodi)
Hebrew, God is gracious

Jordan (Jordyn)
Hebrew, Descendant

Johanna (Joan, Joann, Joanna, Joanne, Johnnie)
Latin, God is gracious

Josephine (Jo, Josefina)
Anglo-Saxon, God shall add

Joy
French, Joy

Joyce
Latin, Merry

Juanita (Juana)
Spanish, God is gracious

Judith (Judy)
Hebrew, Admired

Julia (Julianna, Julie)
Latin, Downy-haired or youthful

June
Latin, From June

Karen (Cara, Kara, Kari)
Greek, Pure

Karina
Nordic, Dear little one

Karla
German, Strong and womanly

Katherine (Cate, Catherine, Cathy, Kate, Kathleen, Kathryn, Kathy, Katie, Kay)
Greek, Pure or virginal

Katrina
German, Pure

Kaya
Native American, My elder sister

Kaylee (Kailey, Kayleigh, Kaylie, Kylee, Kylie)
Celtic/Gaelic, Who is like God?

Kelly (Kelli, Kellie, Kelley)
Celtic/Gaelic, Farm by the spring

Kelsey
Celtic/Gaelic, Island of the ships

Kennedy
Celtic/Gaelic, Helmeted

Kenisha
American, Gorgeous woman

Kiara (Ciara, Kiera)
Celtic/Gaelic, Small and dark

Kimberly (Kim)
Anglo-Saxon, Royal fortress meadow

Kyra (Kira)
Latin, Light

Kristen (Kiersten, Krista, Kristi, Kristie, Kristin, Kristina, Kristine, Kristy)
Greek, Follower of Christ

Krystal (Crystal)
Latin, A clear brilliant glass

Boy

Jacob (Jake, Jakob)
Hebrew, Supplanter

Jaden (Jayden)
Hebrew, God has heard

Jalen (Jaylen, Jaylon)
American, Handsome

Jamal
Arabic, Handsome

James (Jim, Jimmie, Jimmy)
Hebrew, One who replaces

Jared (Jarrett, Jarod)
Hebrew, Down to earth

Jason (Jayson)
Greek, Healer

Javier
Spanish, New house

Jay
Latin, A bird, type of crow

Jeffrey (Geff, Geoff, Geoffrey, Jeff, Jeffery)
Anglo-Saxon, Gift of peace

Jeremy (Jeremiah)
Hebrew, God will uplift

Jerry
Greek, Holy

Jesse (Jess, Jessie)
Hebrew, God exists

Joel
Hebrew, God is willing

John (Jean, Johnnie, Johnny, Juan)
Hebrew, God is gracious and merciful

Jonah
Hebrew, A dove

Jonathan (Johnathan, Jon, Jonathon, Jonny)
Hebrew, Gift of God

Jordan
Hebrew, Descendant

Joseph (Joe, Joey, Jose)
Hebrew, God will increase

Josiah
Hebrew, God has healed

Joshua (Josh)
Hebrew, God saves

Jude
Hebrew, One who is praised

Julius (Julian, Julio)
Greek, Youthful

Justin
French, Just or true

Kaden (Kade, Kadin)
Arabic, Friend or companion

Keaton
Anglo-Saxon, Hawk's town

Keegan
Celtic/Gaelic, Fiery or son of Eagan

Keith
Celtic/Gaelic, Warrior descending

Kelly
Celtic/Gaelic, Warrior or defender

Kendall
Anglo-Saxon, Valley of the river Kent

Kendrick
Celtic/Gaelic, A hill

Kenneth (Ken, Kenny)
Scottish/Gaelic, Born of fire

Kent
Welsh, Bright white

Kerry
Celtic/Gaelic, The dark one

Kevin
Celtic/Gaelic, Handsome or beautiful

Kobe
Hebrew, Supplanter

Kim
Anglo-Saxon, Ruler

Kirk
Native American, From the church

Kurt (Curt, Curtis)
German, Courteous

Kyle
Scottish/Gaelic, From the narrow strait

Girl

Lacey (Lacy)
American, Happy girl

Lana
Polynesian, To float

Latasha (Latascha, Letasha)
American, Joy

Latika
Hindi, Elegant

Laura (Lauren, Laurie, Lauryn, Lora, Loretta, Lori, Lorraine)
Latin, Laurel

Layla (Laila, Leila)
Arabic, Dark beauty

Lee (Leigh)
Anglo-Saxon, Field meadow

Lena
Greek, Light

Leslie (Lesley)
Celtic/Gaelic, Meadow lands

Lillian (Lillie, Lily)
Latin, Lily

Linda (Lynda)
Spanish, Pretty

Lisa
Hebrew, Consecrated to God

Logan
Celtic/Gaelic, Small cove

Lola
Spanish, Strong woman

Louise (Lula)
German, Famous warrior

Lucille (Lucia, Lucy, Luz)
Latin, Light

Lydia
Greek, Beauty

Lynn (Lynette, Lynne)
Latin, Form of Linda or pretty

Mackenzie (Makenzie, Mckenzie)
Celtic/Gaelic, Offspring of Kenneth

Macy (Macey)
Anglo-Saxon, Enduring

Madeline (Madalyn, Madeleine, Madelyn)
Anglo-Saxon, Woman from Magdala

Maddison (Madisyn, Madyson)
Anglo-Saxon, Son or daughter of Matthew

Makayla (Mckayla, Michaela, Mikaela, Mikayla)
Celtic/Gaelic, Who is like God?

Mallory
French, Ill-fated luck

Marcella (Marcia, Marsha)
Latin, Martial

Margaret (Maggie, Maggy, Margarita, Marge, Margie, Marguerite, Peggy)
Persian, Child of light

Maria (Mariah, Marian, Marianne, Marie, Marilyn, Marina, Marion)
Hebrew, Bitter

Marissa (Marisol)
Latin, Of the sea

Mary (Mariana, Maryann, Molly)
Hebrew, Bitter

Maya
Greek, Mother

Mckenna (Makenna)
Celtic/Gaelic, Son or daughter of Ken

Meghan (Meagan, Megan)
Anglo-Saxon, Strong or able

Melanie
Greek, Dark-clothed

Melinda (Mindy)
Greek, Gentle or dark

Melissa
Greek, Bee

Melody
Greek, Song-like

Mercedes
Spanish, Virgin Mary

Michelle (Michele)
French, Who is like a God

Morgan
Welsh, From the sea

Muriel
Latin, Angel of June

Boy

Lamar
Teutonic, Famous around the land

Lamont
Old Norse, A lawyer

Lance
Old French, A lance bearer

Lawrence (Larry, Laurence, Lorenzo)
Latin, From the laurel tree

Lee
Anglo-Saxon, A meadow or clearing

Leland
Anglo-Saxon, From the meadow land

Leo (Leon, Leonard, Leonardo)
Latin, A lion or lionhearted

Leroy
French, The king

Liam
Celtic/Gaelic, Determined guardian

Lionel (Lyonel)
Old French, A young lion

Lloyd
Welsh, Gray-haired

Logan
Scottish/Gaelic, Small cove

Loren (Lorenzo)
Latin, From the laurel tree

Louis (Lewis, Louis, Luis)
Teutonic, A famous warrior

Luke (Luc, Lucas, Lukas)
Greek, Man from Lucania

Luther
Old French, A lute player

Lyle
Old French, From the Island

Mackay
Celtic/Gaelic, Son of the fiery one

Malachi
Hebrew, The messenger of the Lord

Malcolm
Scottish, Follower of St. Columba

Manuel
Spanish, God is with us

Mark (Marc, Marco, Marcus)
Latin, Virile or manly

Marlon
Old French, Wild falcon

Marshall
Teutonic, A horse-keeper

Martin (Marty)
Latin, Warlike

Mason
Old French, A stone mason

Matthew (Mathew, Matt)
Hebrew, A gift of God

Maximilian (Max, Maximus)
Latin, The greatest

Maxwell
Latin, From the stream of Magnus

Michael (Micheal, Miguel, Mike, Mitchell)
Hebrew, Like the Lord

Miles (Myles)
Latin, A soldier

Milton
Anglo-Saxon, From the mill town

Morgan
Welsh, The bright sea

Morris (Maurice, Mauricio, Morrie, Morrison, Morse)
Latin, Dark-skinned, like a Moor

Murphy
Celtic/Gaelic, A warrior of the sea

Murray
Scottish/Gaelic, From the land by the sea

Biblical Names

These names are tried and true, having passed the test of time. They belong to more than one religion and have meanings deeper than the brief descriptions provided here.

Girl

Abilene
Hebrew, Grass

Bethel
Hebrew, House of God

Candace
Latin, Incandescent or white

Carmel
Hebrew, Garden

Delilah
Hebrew, Delicate

Esther (Essie)
Persian, Star

Eve (Eva)
Hebrew, Life giving

Jael
Hebrew, Female goat

Jemima
Hebrew, Dove

Leah
Hebrew, Weary

Lois
Greek, More desirable

Miriam
Hebrew, Longed-for child

Moriah
Hebrew, Seen by God

Ophrah (Ofrah, Ofra)
Hebrew, A fawn

Rachel (Rachael, Raquel)
Hebrew, An ewe

Ruth
Hebrew, Companion or friend

Boy

Adam Hebrew, Mankind	**Judah** Hebrew, Praised
Ariel Hebrew, Lion of God	**Levi** Hebrew, United
Cyrus Greek, Farsighted	**Moses** Egyptian, Drawn out of the water
Elisha Hebrew, God is salvation	**Noah** Hebrew, Rest or peace
Ezekiel Hebrew, God strengthens	**Reuben** Hebrew, Behold: a son
Ezra Hebrew, The helper	**Samson** Hebrew, The sun
Gideon Hebrew, One who fells or hews wood	**Simeon (Shimon)** Hebrew, Harkening or listening
Hiram Hebrew, Exalted brother	**Solomon** Hebrew, Wise and peaceful
Jahzeel Hebrew, God apportions	

Girl

Nadia (Nadie, Nadine)
Russian, Hope

Nadyra
Arabic, Precious

Nancy (Nan, Nandini, Nandita, Nanette, Nanine)
Hebrew, Grace

Nani
Polynesian, Beautiful

Naomi
Hebrew, Sweet or pleasant

Nastasia
Greek, She who will rise again

Natalie (Natalia, Natalya)
Latin, Born on Christmas

Neka
Native American, A wild goose

Nell (Nellie)
French, From the light of the sun

Nevada (Neva)
Spanish, Snow or white as snow

Nevaeh
American, Heaven

Nicole (Nicki, Nicola Nikki)
Greek, Victory of the people

Nimah
Arabic, A blessing or loan

Nina
Hebrew, Grace

Nissa
Scandinavian, A friendly elf

Nita
Native American, A bean grower

Nitika
Native American, Angel

Nona (Noni, Nonie)
Latin, The ninth child

Nora (Norah, Noreen)
Latin, Honor or light

Nyssa
Greek, The beginning

Odelia
Hebrew, I will praise God

Odessa
Greek, A long journey

Odette (Odetta)
French, A home-lover

Odile (Ottilie, Ottoline)
French, Riches or prosperity

Ofelia (Ofilia)
Spanish, A helper or to help

Ohanna
Armenian, God's gracious gift

Okelani (Okalani)
Hawaiian, From Heaven

Oksana
Russian, Glory be to God

Ola
Scandinavian, A descendant or feminine form of Olaf

Olga
Scandinavian, Holy

Olivia (Alivia, Olive)
Greek, Olive tree

Oona
Celtic/Gaelic, Graceful one

Opal
Sanskrit, From the gemstone

Orianna
Greek, Golden one

Boy

Nadir
Arabic, Precious or rare

Narayan (Narayana)
Sanskrit, The son of man

Nathaniel (Nathan)
Hebrew, The gift of God

Ned (Neddie, Neddy)
Anglo-Saxon, A rich protector

Neel
Hindu, Blue

Neil (Neal, Neill)
Celtic/Gaelic, Champion

Nelson
Anglo-Saxon, Son of Neil

Nevada
Spanish, Snow or white

Neville
Old French, From the new town

Nestor
Greek, Traveler

Newton
Anglo-Saxon, From the new town

Nicholas (Nick, Nickolas, Nicolas, Nikolas)
Greek, The victory of the people

Nico (Nicodemus, Nicol)
Italian, Victorious one

Niels
Latin, A horn

Nigel
Latin, Dark or black-haired

Nivens (Niven)
Celtic/Gaelic, Servant of the saints

Noam
Hebrew, Peasant

Noel
French, Christmas

Nolan
Celtic/Gaelic, Champion

Norman (Normand, Norris)
Teutonic, Norseman or ruler

Nyle
Anglo-Saxon, An island

Oakley
Anglo-Saxon, One who lives at the oak tree meadow

Odin
Old Norse, Scandinavian god of war

Olin
Anglo-Saxon, Holly

Oliver
Latin, An olive tree or branch

Omar
Arabic, First born son

Orion
Greek, The son of light

Orlando
Italian, Famed throughout the land

Osborne
Hebrew, Soldier of God

Oscar
Anglo-Saxon, A divine spearman

Otis
Greek, Keen of hearing

Otto
Teutonic, Rich or prosperous

Owen
Welsh, Well-born

Girl

Padma
Sanskrit, A lotus

Paige (Page)
French, Youthful assistant

Pamela (Pam)
Greek, All honey

Patricia (Pat, Patsy, Patti, Patty)
Latin, Of nobility

Paula (Paulette, Pauline)
Latin, Small

Payton (Peyton)
Anglo-Saxon, Village of the warrior

Pearl
Latin, Gem of the sea

Penelope (Penny)
Greek, Weaver

Pepa (Pepita)
Spanish, God shall add

Perry
Anglo-Saxon, The dweller by the pear tree

Phoebe (Phebe)
Greek, Bright shining one

Phyllis
Greek, A leaf

Piper
Anglo-Saxon, Flute player

Placida
Latin, Peaceful or serene

Pomona
Latin, Fertile or fruitful

Priscilla
Latin, Of ancient time

Prudence (Prue)
Latin, Provident or showing careful forethought

Queenie
Anglo-Saxon, Queen or female companion

Quiana
American, Soft, synthetic material

Quincy
Latin, The fifth child

Quinta
Latin, The fifth

Rain
Latin, Ruler

Ramona
Spanish, Mighty or wise

Rana (Ranee, Rani)
Arabic, Beautiful to gaze upon

Ray
French, A stream

Regan
Celtic/Gaelic, Son or daughter of
the small ruler

Rebecca (Becky)
Hebrew, Tied

Rita
Greek, Form of Margarita

Renee
Latin, Reborn

Robin (Robyn)
German, Bright fame

Rhoda
Greek, A rose

Rochelle
French, Little rock

Rhonda (Ronda)
Celtic/Gaelic, Rough Island

Rory
Celtic/Gaelic, The red king

Rhonwen
Welsh, A white lance

Rose (Rosa, Rosalie, Rosie)
Latin, Rosebush

Riley (Reilly, Rylee)
Celtic/Gaelic, A small stream

Roxanne
Persian, Dawn

Risa
Latin, Laughter

Ruby
Latin, A red jewel

Boy

Paco
Native American, Gold eagle

Palmer
Anglo-Saxon, A palm-bearing pilgrim

Parker
Anglo-Saxon, The park-keeper

Patrick (Pat)
Latin, Nobleman

Paul (Paolo, Pablo)
Latin, Small

Percy
Norman, To pierce the valley

Perry
Anglo-Saxon, The dweller by the pear tree

Peter (Pedro, Pete, Pierre)
Greek, A stone or rock

Peyton (Payton)
Anglo-Saxon, A dweller on the warrior's farm

Phillip (Felipe, Phil, Philip)
Greek, A lover of horses

Porter
French, The gatekeeper

Preston
Anglo-Saxon, From the priest's farm

Qimat
Hindi, Valuable

Quade
Latin, Fourth

Quant
French, How much

Quennell
French, Oak tree

Quentin (Quintin, Quinto, Quito)
Latin, The fifth

Quillan
Celtic/Gaelic, Cub

Quin
Celtic/Gaelic, Quintuplet or fifth

Quinlan
Celtic/Gaelic, Very strong

Quinn (Qwin)
Celtic/Gaelic, Fifth

Quon
Chinese, Bright

Rafiq
Arabic, A companion or friend

Rainer (Rainier, Rayner)
Teutonic, A wise warrior

Raleigh
Anglo-Saxon, The meadow of the
Roe deer

Ralph (Raoul, Raul)
Anglo-Saxon, Wolf counselor

Ramsay (Ramsey)
Anglo-Saxon, The island of wild garlic

**Randolph (Randal, Randall,
Randell, Randy)**
Anglo-Saxon, A wolf-like shield

Raymond (Ramiro, Ramon, Ray)
Teutonic, Wise protection

Reardon (Rearden)
Celtic/Gaelic, A royal poet

**Reginald (Reg, Reggie,
Regis, Reynaldo)**
Anglo-Saxon, A wise and powerful ruler

**Richard (Ricardo, Rick,
Rickey, Ricky)**
Teutonic, Brave and strong

Robert (Bob, Bobby, Roberto)
Teutonic, Famous or bright fame

Robin (Robyn)
Anglo-Saxon, A small bird

Rodney
Anglo-Saxon, Land near the water

Roger (Rodger, Rogelio)
Teutonic, A famous spearman

Roland (Rolando)
Teutonic, Famed throughout the land

Ronald (Ron, Ronnie)
Anglo-Saxon, A wise and powerful ruler

Ross
Scottish/Gaelic, A woody meadow

Rudolph (Rodolfo, Rudy)
Teutonic, A famous wolf

Ryan
Celtic/Gaelic, A little king

Celebrity Names

Could Marilyn Monroe have achieved fame as Norma Jean Mortenson? Start your child off with a stellar name and he or she will be destined for greatness from the start.

Girl

Calista (Calista Flockhart)
Greek, Beautiful

Celine (Celine Dion)
French, Moon

Demi (Demi Moore)
Greek, Half or small

Goldie (Goldie Hawn)
Anglo-Saxon, The golden one

Gwyneth (Gwyneth Paltrow)
Welsh, From a region of North Wales

Jamie (Jamie Lee Curtis)
Celtic/Gaelic, One who replaces

Jewel (Jewel Kilchner)
Latin, Joy

Latoya (Latoya Jackson)
African-American, Praised woman

Leelee (Leelee Sobieski)
Sanskrit, Playful one

Milla (Milla Jovovich)
Teutonic, Strong and industrious

Reba (Reba Mcintyre)
Hebrew, A knotted cord

Reese (Reese Witherspoon)
Welsh, Ardent one

Salma (Salma Hayek)
Hebrew, Peace

Shania (Shania Twain)
Celtic/Gaelic, God is gracious

Sigourney (Sigourney Weaver)
Old Norse, The conqueror

Whoopi (Whoopi Goldberg)
British, Shout of delight

Boy

Antonio (Antonio Banderas)
Spanish, Worthy of praise

Benicio (Benicio Del Toro)
Spanish, Blessed

Clint (Clint Eastwood)
Anglo-Saxon, The place on the headland

Cuba (Cuba Gooding Jr.)
Spanish, For the country

Emilio (Emilio Estevez)
Spanish, Industrious

Heath (Heath Ledger)
Anglo-Saxon, Wasteland

**Jean Claude
(Jean Claude Van Damme)**
French, God is gracious and victorious

Jude (Jude Law)
Hebrew, Praise

Kelsey (Kelsey Grammer)
Old Norse, A dweller on the island

Marlon (Marlon Brando)
Old French, Wild falcon

Phoenix (Joaquin Phoenix)
Greek, The legendary bird that rises from its own ashes

Russell (Russell Crowe)
Old French, Redhead

Skeet (Skeet Ulrich)
Anglo-Saxon, Speedy

Sylvester (Sylvester Stallone)
Latin, From the forest

Vince (Vince Vaughn)
Latin, Victor

Woody (Woody Allen)
Anglo-Saxon, The path through the woods

Girl

Sabrina
Latin, From the border

Samantha
Hebrew, Listener of God

Sandra (Sandy)
Greek, Helper and defender of mankind

Sarah (Sadie, Sally, Sara)
Anglo-Saxon, Princess

Savannah (Savanna)
Spanish, Treeless plain

Shania
Native American, I'm on my way

Shannon
Celtic/Gaelic, Wise one

Sharon
Hebrew, Princess

Sheila (Shelia)
Latin, Blind

Shelby
Anglo-Saxon, A sheltered town

Sherry (Cheri, Shari, Sheri, Sherri, Sherrie)
French, Beloved

Sidney
Anglo-Saxon, From the riverside meadow

Sierra (Cierra)
Spanish, Saw-toothed mountain range

Skylar (Skyler)
Nordic, Learned one

Sonia (Sonja, Sonya)
Greek, Wisdom

Sophia (Sophie)
Greek, Wisdom

Stacey (Stacie, Stacy)
Greek, Resurrection

Stella
Latin, Star

Stephanie (Stefania, Stefanie)
Greek, Crown

Susan (Sue, Susanna, Susie, Suzanne)
Hebrew, Lily

Sylvia (Silvia)
Latin, Woodland

Tabitha
Aramaic, Gazelle

Tamara (Tami, Tammie, Tammy)
Hebrew, Palm tree

Tamiko
Japanese, Child of Tami

Tanya
Greek, Sun

Tara
Celtic/Gaelic, Tower or crag

Tasha (form of Natasha)
Latin, Born at Christmas

Tatyana (Tatiana)
Latin, Silver-haired

Teri (Terri, Terry)
Latin, Female form of Terence

Tessa
Greek, Gatherer

Thelma
Greek, Nursling

Theresa (Teresa)
Latin, Harvester

Tiffany
Greek, Appearance of God

Tina
Latin, Nickname for names ending in "tine"

Toni (Tonya)
Latin, Female form of Anthony

Tracy (Tracey, Traci)
Anglo-Saxon, Brave

Tricia
Latin, Form of Patricia, or nobility

Trinity
American, Holy three

Tyler
Anglo-Saxon, House builder

Boy

Salvatore (Salvador)
Italian, Savior

Samuel (Sam, Sammy)
Hebrew, Asked of God

Santiago
Spanish, Of Saint James

Santos
Spanish, Of the saints

Saul
Hebrew, Asked or prayed for

Sawyer
Anglo-Saxon, A sawer of wood

Scott
Anglo-Saxon, Of Scottish origin

Sebastian
Latin, Venerable

Sedgely
Anglo-Saxon, From the warrior's meadow

Sergio
Italian, Attendant

Seth
Hebrew, The appointed one

Shannon
Celtic/Gaelic, From the river in Ireland

Shaun (Sean, Shane, Shawn)
Celtic/Gaelic, God is gracious

Sheldon
Anglo-Saxon, From the steep valley

Sherman
Anglo-Saxon, Shearer or servant

Sidney
Anglo-Saxon, From the riverside meadow

Simon
Hebrew, The listener

Skyler (Schuyler, Skylar)
Dutch, A shield or scholar

Spencer
Old French, A dispenser of provisions

Stanley
Anglo-Saxon, Rocky meadow

Stephen (Stefan, Stefanos, Steffan, Stephan, Stephano, Steve, Steven)
Teutonic, A crown or garland

Stuart (Stewart, Stu)
Anglo-Saxon, A steward or keeper of a household

Tanner (Tannar)
Anglo-Saxon, A leather worker

Tate
Old Norse, Cheerful or jolly

Terrell
Anglo-Saxon, Thunderer

Terrence (Terence, Terrance, Terry)
Latin, Tender and gracious

Theodore (Ted, Teddy)
Greek, Divine gift

Thomas (Tom, Tomas, Tommie, Tommy)
Greek, A twin

Timothy (Tim, Timmy)
Greek, Honoring God or honored by God

Toby (Tobie)
Hebrew, The Lord is good

Todd (Tod)
Old Norse, A fox or fox hunter

Tracy
Anglo-Saxon, Brave

Travis
French, Crossroads

Trent
German, Thirty

Trevor
Celtic/Gaelic, Prudent

Tristen (Tristan, Triston, Tristam)
Celtic/Gaelic, Sadness

Troy
Celtic/Gaelic, Descendant of the foot soldier

Tybalt (Theobald)
Teutonic, Brave people

Tyrese (Tyrus)
Latin, A person from Tyre (Africa)

Tyrone
Celtic/Gaelic, Land of Owen or younger soldier

Girl

Ula
Celtic/Gaelic, Sea jewel

Ulla
German, To fill up

Ulani
Polynesian, Cheerful or light-hearted

Ulrika (Ulrike)
Scandinavian, Ruler over all

Ultima
Latin, Aloof

Uma
Hebrew, Nation

Ummi
African, My mother

Una
Latin, One

Undine
Latin, Of the wave

Unity
Latin, Oneness

Urania
Greek, Heavenly, muse of astronomy

Uria
Hebrew, Light of the Lord

Ursula (Ursa, Ursala)
Latin, Female bear

Uta (Ute)
German, Fortunate maid of battle

Utah
American, From the state

Utina
Native American, A woman of my country

Vala
Anglo-Saxon, Chosen

Valda
Scandinavian, Spirited warrior

Valencia
Latin, Bravery

Valentina
Latin, Strong and healthy

Valerie (Val, Valarie, Valeria)
Latin, Strong

Valora
Latin, The valorous

Vanessa
Greek, Butterfly

Vanya
Russian, Gracious gift of God

Veda
Sanskrit, Wisdom and knowledge

Vega
Arabic, A falling star

Velma
Teutonic, Female form of William

Velvet
Anglo-Saxon, As soft as velvet

Vera
Latin, True

Verena
Teutonic, Defender

Verity
Latin, Truth

Verna
Latin, Truth

Veronica
Latin, True victory

Verran
Cornish, The short one

Vesta
Latin, Goddess of the hearth

Victoria (Vicki, Vickie, Vicky, Tori)
Latin, Victory

Virginia (Ginnie, Ginny)
Latin, Maiden or virgin

Vita
Latin, Life

Vivian (Vivi, Vivienne)
Latin, Alive

Vondra
Slavic, The love of a woman

Boy

Ugo
Italian, Heart and mind

Uriel
Latin, Light

Ulf
Swedish, Wolf-like

Urson
French, Little bear

Ulrich
Teutonic, A ruler

Utah
American, From the state

Ulysses
Greek, The angry one or wrathful

Uwan
Aboriginal, To meet

Umar
Arabic, Flourishing or long-lived

Vadim
Russian, A powerful ruler

Umberto
Italian, A famous warrior

Vail
Anglo-Saxon, From the valley

Upton
Anglo-Saxon, From the upper farm

Valentine (Valentin, Valentino)
Latin, Strong or healthy

Uriah (Uri)
Russian, God is light

Valeray
Old French, Valor or strength

Van
Dutch, God is good

Vered
Hebrew, A rose

Vance
Anglo-Saxon, A thresher

Verner
Scandinavian, The protecting army

Vane
Anglo-Saxon, From the marsh or fen

Vernon
Latin, Spring-like or youthful

Vanya
Russian, God is great

Victor
Latin, Winner or conqueror

Varden
French, From the green hills

Vinay
Hindu, Good behavior

Varian
Latin, The changeable one

Vincent (Vicente, Vinnie, Vinny)
Latin, He who defeats

Varick
Icelandic, A sea drifter

Virgil
Latin, Strong

Vartan
Armenian, A rose

Vitale
Latin, Lively

Varun
Hindu, Lord of the waters

Vito
Latin, Conqueror

Varuna
Sanskrit, God of the night sky

Vitus
Latin, Life

Vasily
Russian, Royal or kingly

Vivian
Latin, Gracious in life

Vaughan
Welsh, Small

Vladimir
Slavic, Prince or powerful ruler

Volker
Teutonic, Of the people

Presidential Names

*One of the things that makes this country great
is that every child grows up believing that he or
she may later become President. With one
of these names, he or she is made for the role!*

Girl

**Abigail (Abigail Adams,
2nd First Lady)**
Teutonic, Exalted father

**Dolley (Dolley Madison,
4th First Lady)**
American, Gift of God

**Eleanor (Eleanor Roosevelt,
32nd First Lady)**
Greek, Light

**Frances (Frances Cleveland,
22nd & 24th First Lady)**
Latin, From France

**Ida (Ida Mckinley,
25th First Lady)**
British, Prosperous

**Jacqueline (Jacqueline
Kennedy, 35th First Lady)**
French, One who supplants

**Kennedy (John Fitzgerald
Kennedy, 35th President)**
Celtic/Gaelic, Helmeted

**Louisa (Louisa Adams,
6th First Lady)**
Teutonic, Famous warrior

**Lucretia (Lucretia Garfield,
20th First Lady)**
Latin, Succeed

**Lucy (Lucy Hayes,
19th First Lady)**
Latin, Light

**Madison (James Madison,
4th President)**
Anglo-Saxon, Son or daughter of
Matthew

**Martha (Martha Washington,
1st First Lady and Martha
Jefferson, 3rd First Lady)**
Aramaic, Lady

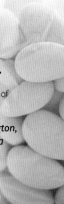

Boy

Reagan (Ronald Reagan, 40th President)
Celtic/Gaelic, Son or daughter of the small ruler

Taylor (Zachary Taylor, 12th President)
British, Tailor

Carter (Jimmy Carter, 39th President)
Old French, Transporter

Chester (Chester A. Arthur, 21st President)
Latin, Legionary camp

Clinton (Bill Clinton, 42nd President)
Anglo-Saxon, Fenced settlement

Fitzgerald (John Fitzgerald Kennedy, 35th President)
Old French, Son of Gerald

Grant (Ulysses S. Grant, 18th President)
Celtic/Gaelic, Great

Grover (Grover Cleveland, 22nd & 24th President)
Anglo-Saxon, One living by a grove

Harrison (William Henry Harrison, 9th President)
Anglo-Saxon, Son of Harry

Howard (William Howard Taft, 27th President)
Anglo-Saxon, Guardian of the home

Jackson (Andrew Jackson, 7th President)
Anglo-Saxon, Son of Jack

Jefferson (Thomas Jefferson, 3rd President)
Anglo-Saxon, Peaceful god

Pierce (Franklin Pierce, 14th President)
Anglo-Saxon, Rock

Quincy (John Quincy Adams, 6th President)
French, Fifth son's world

Theodore (Theodore Roosevelt, 26th President)
Anglo-Saxon, God's gift

Tyler (John Tyler, 10th President)
Anglo-Saxon, House builder

Girl

Wallis
Anglo-Saxon, Woman from France

Wanda
German, Kindred

Wednesday
Anglo-Saxon, From the weekday

Wendy (Wenda, Wendi)
Anglo-Saxon, Fair one

Whitney
Anglo-Saxon, White island

Willa
Teutonic, Protector

Williemae (Willie Mae)
American, Protector of spring

Wilma
Teutonic, Caretaker

Winifred
Teutonic, Friend of peace

Winona (Wynona)
Native American, First-born daughter

Winter
Anglo-Saxon, Born in the winter months

Wren
Anglo-Saxon, A tiny bird

Xamira
Persian, Diamond

Xena
Greek, Welcome guest

Xuan
Chinese, Spring

Yamuna
Hindi, A sacred river

Yasmin (Yasmeen, Yasmin, Yasmina, Yasmine)
Arabic, Jasmine

Yelena
Russian, Bright one

Yoko
Japanese, Positive child, female

Yolanda
Latin, Violet flower

Yvonne (Yvette)
French, Archer

Zelda
Teutonic, Female warrior

Zenobia
Greek, Given life by Zeus

Ziva
Hebrew, Aglow or splendor

Zizi
Hungarian, Dedicated to God

Zoe (Zoey)
Greek, Life

Zola
Italian, Ball of earth

Zora
Greek, Dawn

Zulaykha (Zuleikha)
Arabic, Potiphar's wife

Boy

Wade
Anglo-Saxon, A wanderer

Waldo
Anglo-Saxon, God's power

Walker
Anglo-Saxon, A fuller or one who
thickens cloth

Wallace
Old French, A foreigner

Walter
Teutonic, An army general

Warren
Old French, To preserve

Wayne
Anglo-Saxon, A cart or wagon
maker

Wendell
Teutonic, Valley or wanderer

Wesley
Anglo-Saxon, The west meadow

Weston
Anglo-Saxon, From the western
farm or town

Wilbur
Anglo-Saxon, The resolute one

Wilfred
Teutonic, Desirous of peace or
peacemaker

Wilkes
Anglo-Saxon, A strong and resolute
protector

Willard
Anglo-Saxon, Resolute and brave

**William (Bill, Billie, Billy,
Guillermo, Will, Willie, Willis)**
Teutonic, A strong and resolute
protector

Willoughby
Old Norse, From the farm by
the willows

Wilson
Anglo-Saxon, The son of William

Winston
Anglo-Saxon, Victory town

Wolfgang
Teutonic, Path of a wolf

Wyatt
Teutonic, The wide one

Xanthus
Greek, Golden-haired

Xavier
Arabic, Bright

Xenos
Greek, Stranger

Xerxes
Persian, King or ruler

Yael
Hebrew, A wild goat

Yale
Anglo-Saxon, From the corner of the land

Yan
Hebrew, God is grace

Yardley
Anglo-Saxon, From the enclosed meadow

Yates
Anglo-Saxon, The keeper of the gates

Yehuda (Yehudi)
Hebrew, The praised one

Yevgeni
Russian, The noble, well-born one

Yitzaak (Yitzak)
Hebrew, The laughing one

Yosef
Hebrew, God shall add

Yves
French, The little archer

Zachariah
Hebrew, Remembered by God

Zachary (Zackary, Zachery, Zackery)
Hebrew, The Lord has remembered

Zane
Hebrew, God is gracious

Zion
Hebrew, A sigh

Ziggy
Slavic, To get rid of anger

Zubin
Hebrew, The exalted one

Resources

Other resources for finding baby names:

Your personal family tree

Many couples are afraid to get family input on names, fearing that Aunt Lucille or Cousin David will be hurt that you don't choose his or her name. Try a less direct approach at a family gathering by asking each person to tell a story about his favorite relative who is no longer living. Even if you don't unearth a name for baby, you will undoubtedly learn more about your family and what makes it special.

Baby Center

www.babycenter.com/babyname

Popular baby name database searchable by alphabet, sex, ethnic origin, number of syllables, and more. Provides guidelines on issues to consider when naming a baby, lists of the most popular baby names from 1880 to the present day, and a customized name poll to share with your friends.

Baby Name Network

www.babynamenetwork.com/index.cfm

A database containing thousands of baby names of many different origins—from Aboriginal to Zimbabwean—searchable by alphabet, origin, or name.

Baby Names.com

www.babynames.com/V5/index.php

A database of over 6,000 names searchable by alphabet or name, includes lists of top names for the past three years, message boards for group interests, and articles on topics of parenthood.

Names Through the Ages by Teresa Norman. New York: Berkley Pub, 1999.

A person's name conveys a culture, a history, and a way of looking at the world. And as centuries of war, immigration, rulers, and religions have changed a country, they have also changed the names of its people. This unusual book traces the history of Europe, from the ancient Roman era to the present, and shows how names originated and changed throughout the ages.

Picture Credits

Photography by Debi Treloar (unless stated otherwise)

Caroline Arber **2, 54** center below
David Brittain **29**
Polly Wreford **34, 53**

32 Vincent & Frieda Plasschaert's house in Brügge, Belgium

Acknowledgments

With many thanks to all our little models:

Amber, Antonia, Darcey, Erin, Jessica,

Max, Sorcha, and Tobey

All wooden toys courtesy of Oggetti,

135 & 143 Fulham Road, London SW3